Crossings 22

Meditations in the Feminine

Meditations in the Feminine

Michela Zanarella

Translated from the Italian by

Leanne Hoppe

Bordighera Press

Library of Congress Control Number: 2017959135

Printed in the United States.

Published by
BORDIGHERA PRESS
John D. Calandra Italian American Institute
25 West 43rd Street, 17th Floor
New York, NY 10036

CROSSINGS 22
ISBN 978-1-59954-110-5

Contents

Preface

Wthat appears straightforward often is not. I began this project in the beginning of 2013 with an email for permission to translate *Meditazioni al Femminile*. Zanarella obliged, and we began our collaboration. I chose to begin with this volume because of its title, wondering what does it mean, Meditations in the Feminine? The poems that follow establish grounds and remove them.

The title poem, "Meditations in the Feminine" demonstrates the angle. The word doesn't work on its own—*meditazioni* has a masculine ending—the gendered nouns of a romance language. Thus, Zanarella clarifies. But the explanation isn't easy—what are meditations in the feminine? Are they female meditations? Not quite. Zanarella writes:

> In a pleasant skin
> I find myself
> . . .
> The sky and the love
> satisfy my breath
> after a privilege
> divine to life.

Here, the reader encounters the female as divinity: she's not angry, she's sacred. The next poem in the volume undoes it:

> Too brief the sense
> and the nature of a breath.
> We are a small buzzing
> underneath eternities.

No longer divine, left with the momentary, the human. It's that oscillation that makes the volume masterful. Earlier in the volume, the speaker nearly imagines herself a divinity in "As a Venus." Zanarella writes, "I made the sky love me / as a Venus clinging to the winds." The speaker limits the dream to a simile and lowercases venus to avoid the divine—she's content to "put on the light" and sing "in choir hymns to life." At the same time, the syntax of the line reveals the speaker's power: the action occurs before the qualification. The speaker leads the reader in between two realms. And Venus, or venus, clings to the winds—she's grasping motion.

The qualifying becomes more clear in "Mud and Roots." The poem begins, "We smother our miseries / with tears." The line thrusts the reader back into the earthly, the fundamentally human. No longer elevated, the poem continues: "We seek the judgment of God." But there's beauty here, too: "We meet in the bosom of the same earth, / mud and roots / for a new sprout." Only by existing within bounds, within the real and what appears dirty, is there new growth. The poet makes it her task to reveal this through a variety of subjects, moving among poems of love, elegy, ekphrasis, confession . . .

The oscillation continues, moving between the local and the national. The poet contemplates the Gianicolo Fountain in Rome as a place of familiarity in "Ancient Horizon (at the Gianicolo Fountain)." Zanarella writes, "I reveal sovereignties of solitude / and I bring myself to the fingers the wisdom" where the surrounding growth "protects all my naivety." Zanarella, who was born in Padua, moved to Rome as an adult, and this perhaps shapes her experience of the antiquity of the scene. Here the speaker connects with what it means to be an outsider, to the awe that one can experience by not having always known a landscape. The poet makes the fountain the active force in the poem: she, naïve, experiences it. Unsettled, the poet moves outward in the next poem—to "Italy," a poem that's more sure of itself, more comfortable. Where in "Ancient Horizon," the speaker acts more passively, as shown by lines that begin, "He welcomes me" and "I experience," in "Italy" the speaker demonstrates authority:

> I speak of homeland,
> as of a green mother,
> she revolts against white melancholies of fog,
> I break red edges of sap
> and inhale
> energy from the past.

And rightfully so. It's natural to exercise caution over what one can't claim ownership of. Though most of the poems in the volume rely on a present speaker, Zanarella balances passivity with action through careful choices in the syntax of verbs, in the presence of the I.

In the next poem, the focus remains global. Here again, the speaker takes action. Zanarella writes:

I feel your white tunic

. . .

I know how to find you.

The universality of the subject matter doesn't halt readers' understanding of volume's raison d'être. In fact, in "Giovanni Paolo II" the predominant motifs of the volume intersect. The poem begins with the natural: "My young cheeks / on bare feet across the seasons." The respect offered to Giovanni Paolo II parallels expressions found in the volume's love poems: "I know how you find you / secret in my blood." The speaker hints at the divine: "prayers and fragrances of eternity. / In sacred conventions of life." And then there's the national, most obviously, which emerges through the subject and global perspective: "I feel your white tunic / still in the knees of the world / and one thousand eyes offering you gratitude." It's appropriate for these motifs to appear together in a poem whose subject is a figure that transcends the national. The lens is wide enough to allow the interaction of genre, and the subject matter speaks to what can be both intensely personal, and, at the same time, public. The speaker in *Meditations in the Feminine* seeks to balance these priorities, to examine the world with all of herself.

As suddenly as this wholeness appears, it's removed. The lens narrows in the following poem, "Monteverde and my Cheeks," opening again in Rome: "The prompt elm trees / of Ozanam road." The focus narrows further: "At a crossroads, / Monteverde and my cheeks." Here, the reader cinematically sees less and less of the outer landscape to turn inward on the speaker. The order of this sequence doesn't only create variety; Zanarella mimics natural order. A person cannot always exercise control over what's outside oneself, and, likewise, authority, or familiarity, can be comfortable and can allow one more freedom to speak honestly.

This movement creates fluidity in the volume while also allowing for intersections that surprise the reader. The actions of the speaker mimic one's interactions with the world, the self-discovery that so many poets lead readers through, tuned up a key, to the feminine ending. What follows are poems that fall into the canon somewhere between personal and pastoral, that draw the reader to challenge her ideas about what creates a voice, how nature connects to our senses, to our being.

Meditations in the Feminine

Lapilli di vita

In queste ossa
viaggio
e insieme mi porto
lapilli di vita.
Scavo calore
consumo il fiato,
amo.
Voglio andare
con la pelle
a restare
magìa
nel destino.
Voglio esplodere
di te
e sapere il sapore
del mare.

Sparks of Life

In these bones
I travel
and I carry with me
the little sparks of life.
I unearth heat,
take in breath,
I love.
I want
to stay in this skin,
I want it to remain
magic
in destiny.
I want you to erupt
out of me
and I want to know
the taste of the sea.

M'incateno alle origini

M'incateno alle origini
della luce,
disfo un tramonto
appena poesia mi tocca,
creo con le labbra la sorte
di un orizzonte che esalta
umane villeggiature d'ossa.
Mi riposo nell'improvviso vibrare
di nuvola,
incrociando fiumi di silenzio
all'estroso azzurro di un popolo
d'istanti.
Incarnata nell'esilio
di terra ed acqua
mi allaccio al vento, m'abbandono al fuoco.
Ad occhi pieni di mondo
intorno al sole
passo immobile ad esistere
e come Dafne,
eterna mi faccio bosco d'ulivi.

I Chain Myself to the Origins

I chain myself to the origins
of light,
I undo a sunset
just as poetry touches me,
with my lips I create the fate
of a horizon that glorifies
cemeteries filled with bones.
I rest in the sudden vibration
of a cloud,
intersecting rivers of silence
at the whimsical azure of a crowd
of instants.
Embodied in the exile
of earth and water,
I bind myself to the wind, I yield to the flames.
To eyes permeated by the world
surrounding the sun,
I make myself eternal
and like Daphne, I make myself
a forest of olive trees.

Un rossore di favola e di fiato

Mi muovo
come petalo di luce,
esclamando al cielo
morsi d'amore.
Ho sulla fronte
il chiasso delle tue labbra,
attendo sillabe
come sigillo ad una notte eterna.
Ho spinto l'anima
addosso ai tuoi vapori
quasi a viziare le mie rotaie
di tremore.
Mi fai rispondere alla vita
con un rossore di favola e di fiato.
In uno scroscio di falangi
l'emozione mi trova nuda
ed avida di tutto.
E dimenticando il tempo
in ascolto,
mi stropiccio nei tuoi sensi
già invasi dal destino.

A Blush of Fable and of Breath

I move
as a petal of light,
shouting the pains of love
at the sky.
I have on my brow
the uproar of your lips,
I attend to syllables
as a seal to the eternal night.
I pushed my soul
on your vapors
almost to spoil my tracks
of tremors.
You make me respond to life
with a blush of fable and of breath.
In a roar of phalanxes
emotion finds me naked
and greedy of everything.
And forgetting the time
in listening,
I drag myself in your senses
already invaded by destiny.

Sguardi d'agosto

Mi cerchi
in sguardi d'agosto
getti il tuo azzurro
a bordo delle mie labbra.
Consegni ad eternità
un pulsare di muscoli e luce
ti fai elettricità dove i sudori
sanno di resina e mare.
Invadi di vita
la mia vita
e con la retina
mi chiami amore.

August's Glances

You seek me
in glances of August,
you throw your blue
on the edges of my lips.
You commit a pulse
of muscles and light to eternity,
you become electricity where sweat
smells of resin and sea.
You invade my life
with life
and with the retina
you call me love.

Passione che non passa

Il mio amare
nelle strade, nelle viscere
nel silenzio tutto il tuo esistere,
mi fa sentire gli angoli di un paradiso
addosso.
La voce azzurra del destino
mi lascia come una bambina
a sognare i rumori dolci
dei tuoi segreti.
La mia vita ha senso
nell'aria nuda che tocchiamo
insieme,
nella geometria di orizzonti
che giocano a tramonto perfetto,
in quell'eco di emozioni
illuminate da un tempo assente.
Su noi,
come sul mare le acque
di quell che siamo,
passione che non passa.

Passion That Does Not Pass

My love
in the streets, in the entrails,
in silence, all your existence
makes me feel the corners of a paradise
above.
The azure voice of destiny
leaves me as a child
to dream sweet rumors
of your secrets.
My life has meaning
in the naked air that we touch
together,
in the geometry of horizons
that play at perfect descent,
in that echo of emotions
illuminated from an absent time.
On us,
as on the sea, the waters
of which we are,
passion that does not pass.

Insieme oltre

Sogno un altrove
un respirare
nuvole ed eterno
a nutrire la schiena
di vapori ancora intatti,
ancora nostri.
Insieme
oltre gli schemi della fine,
ci spingeremo alati
sulle assi del tempo,
come a scoprirci nudi
per la prima volta,
nervosi d'amore,
pronti a scavare intimità
d'acque e universo.
Non svaniranno le falangi
in fiamme,
non morirà il sudore avido
di gioco,
consumeremo il cielo
gocciolando innamorati sui marciapiedi
del destino.
Fradici di sensi
esisteremo anche
dove assente è l'infinito.

Together Beyond

Dream an elsewhere,
a breathing in
clouds and eternity
to nourish the back,
of vapors still intact,
still ours.
Together,
beyond the outlines of the end,
we will push winged
on the axes of time,
as discovering ourselves naked
for the first time,
nervous because of love,
ready to unearth intimacy
of waters and universe.
The phalanxes will not vanish
in flames,
the greedy sweat of play
will not die,
we will consume the sky
dripping in love on the sidewalks
of destiny.
Drenched by sensuality
we too will exist
where the infinite is absent.

Tramonto padovano

Mentre il fieno parla
la mia cornea ti va a cercare
nel peso di un confine.
Sento fin troppa lontananza
ed una smania d'amore
in ogni nuvola.
Ma in cuore possiedo
un piazzale caldo d'emozioni,
un sogno ed una promessa a Dio.
Sembrano i tuoi occhi
le pianure deliziose della mia terra,
le umide avidità di un fiume
che spia estate e paesi.
É come se nelle pieghe rosse
di un tramonto padovano,
la tua voce camminasse
per migliaia di volte
dentro le mie stanze,
nei miei angoli di vita.
Col privilegio
di farsi ventaglio di poesia
e vizio di dolcezza.

Paduan Sunset

While the hay speaks
my cornea goes looking for you
in the burden of a boundary.
I feel too much distance
and a frenzy of love
in every cloud.
But in the heart I own
a hot plaza of emotions,
a dream and a promise to God.
Your eyes seem like the
delicious plains of my land,
the damp greed of a river
that spies on summers and countries.
It's as in the red folds
of a Paduan sunset,
your voice walked
for thousands of times
inside my quarters,
in my corners of life.
With the benefit
of becoming a fan of poetry
and vice of sweetness.

Uno spazio nell'alba

Mi trovo in felici fiumi d'amore
a dondolare caldi respiri di silenzio.
Si posano in vena
veloci notti ed archi di dolcezza.
Dammi luce e polline vivo
in forma di brivido,
tu che sei uomo e arcipelago in trasparenza
sul mio seno.
Nel curvare liscio di schiene e profumo,
il destino è già pioggia,
memoria d'azzurro maturo.
E il nostro volto
uno spazio nell'alba.

A Space in the Dawn

I find myself in happy rivers of love
rocking warm breaths of silence.
They settle in the vein,
fleeting nights and arches of gentleness.
Give me light and living pollen
in the form of shivering,
you that are man and a transparent archipelago
on my breast.
In the curving of smooth backs and perfume,
destiny is already raining
the memory of ripe blue.
And our face,
a space in the dawn.

Antichi suoni d'amore

L'istante di un sospiro
si aggrappa all'anima
allagando gli occhi
di segreti.
É il cuore
che salta in cielo
a pochi passi dall'eterno.
Percorre lunghi sentieri
di felicità
e si ferma a sciogliere
le pelli sotto gli echi
della sera.
Mentre il tramonto
resta una mano tremante
d'emozione,
le labbra danzano tra loro
e s'inebriano,
di vertebre tese
a trovare quel cielo lontano
che ha strappato i silenzi
per rievocare antichi suoni d'amore.
E continuano a correre
le voci
risorgendo sole al mattino.

Ancient Sounds of Love

The instant of a sigh
grasps onto the soul
flooding the eyes
with secrets.
It is the heart
which jumps in the sky
to a few steps from eternity.
It travels long paths
of happiness
and stops to melt
the skins underneath the echoes
of the evening.
While the sunset
stays a trembling hand
of emotion,
the lips dance between themselves
and inebriate themselves
of tense vertebrae
to locate that faraway sky
that has torn silences
in order to recall ancient sounds of love.
And they continue to run
the voices
resurrecting sun to the morning.

Mongolfiere

Una lacrima cresce tra le mani,
diventa fiume in corsa nelle vene
appena ti allontani.
Non vivo senza il chiaro dei tuoi risvegli,
quando mi baci prima di partire
e stringi il cuscino per annusare l'odore
che ci ha unito nell'infinito.
Ho ascoltato il canto delle serrature
fingendo che fosse solo musica,
ho visto il tuo sorriso svanire
dietro gli angoli d'uno sbadiglio.
Dormo ancora.
Appari dentro i colori d'un arcobaleno
voli nelle mongolfiere dell'anima,
spargi coriandoli di vita dalle sponde del cielo,
accompagni un bimbo al parco della giovinezza,
un uomo abbracciato alla propria immagine
che gioca con palloni di luce
nelle strade bianche della libertà.
Il sogno respira la mia mente.
Trovo una pagina di terra da riempire,
scrivo col fiato qualche domanda,
chiudo gli occhi
e parlo di te alla solitudine.

Hot-Air Balloons

A tear grows between the hands,
it becomes a stream in motion in the veins
as you separate yourself.
I do not live without the bright of your awakening,
when you kiss me before leaving
and you cling to the pillow for the smell
that has joined us in the infinite.
I heard the song of the locks,
imagining that it was only music,
I saw your smile vanish
behind the angles of a yawn.
I sleep yet.
You appear inside the colors of a rainbow,
you fly in hot-air balloons of the spirit,
you scatter confetti of life from the banks of heaven,
you accompany a child to the gardens of youth,
a man nestled to the typical image
that plays with balls of light
in the white streets of freedom.
The dream inhales my intellect.
I find a page of ground to fill,
I write with the breath some question,
I shut the eyes
and I speak of you to the solitude.

Arcobaleni e rugiade

Dove il fiato mi consente
pettino i giorni con un sorriso.
Assorta ad inseguire sogni
come una vita,
con il silenzio dell'anima
provo a fermare i binari
del tempo,
fino a fingermi fioca luce
nel grembo dell'eternità.
Solo un fischio di luna
srotola il mio vagare tra i cieli
e mi riporta
tra le geometrie di terra,
stanca, ad incontrare la realtà.
Sfoglio i grigiori di città
tra arie incattivite da nebbie sporche
ed esistenze ammuffite
nel chiasso e nella velocità.
Mentre i fiumi esplodono
ed i ghiacci si consumano,
con gli occhi infangati di rabbia
cerco un po' di calma
nel mio mondo ancora immacolato.
Arcobaleni e rugiade
hanno la mia voce.

Rainbows and Dew

Where the breath allows me
I comb the days with a smile.
Absorbed by chasing dreams
as a life,
with silence of the soul
I try to stop the tracks
of time,
I will put an end to pretending to be feeble light
in the lap of eternity.
Only a whistle of the moon
unrolls my wanderings among the heavens
and brings back to me
between the geometries of the earth,
stagnant, to meeting the reality.
I browse the grayness of the city
through songs in captivity of filthy hazes
and molded existences
in noise and in speed.
While rivers burst forth
and ices are consumed,
with eyes stained by anger
I look for a bit of calm
in my world still immaculate.
Rainbows and dew:
they have my voice.

Calde piume

Sintesi di luci imprigionate
nel lento tintinnio d'ormeggi.
Manovre costanti di vento
spingono le vele verso un podio
azzurro
in fusione perfetta col mare.
Gruppi di gabbiani
giocano tra cerchi di sabbia,
sfidando le mutevoli forme
capricciose del sole.
Ali di paradiso,
giganti messaggeri del silenzio
indispettiti dal vocio parallelo
d'altri esploratori d'acque,
lanciano grida convulse
alla conquista di terre lontane.
Trionfa il volo verso l'ignoto.
Oltre le nuvole
tramonti scelti,
destini conclusi,
amori protetti
da calde piume di neve.

Hot Plumes

Synthesis of imprisoned lights
in the slow jingling of moorings.
Steady drives of wind
they push the sails toward
an azure podium
in perfect fusion with the sea.
Packs of seagulls
playing among circles of sand,
challenging fickle forms,
whimsical of the sun.
Wings of paradise,
giant messengers of silence
you get annoyed by a parallel bawl
of the next explorers of waters,
they throw cries unrestrained
to the conquest of distant lands.
Triumph, the flight direction unknown.
Beyond the clouds
sunsets chosen
destinies concluded,
loves protected
in the hot plumes of snow.

Come una venere

Mi apparve muta la sera
in una carezza scura di attimi.
Le sue braccia mi raccolsero
dal profumo del giorno
e mi condussero in una terra
che spiava i sogni e le nuvole.
Sguardi d'angelo
cercavano il mio respiro
per spingere lontano cuori spenti
e lacrime mascherate di gioia.
Indossai la luce
e mi lasciai tuffare tra i rami
ed il grano.
Cantai in coro lodi alla vita
tra il pullulare di polline
e resine.
Mi feci amare dal cielo
come una venere aggrappata
ai venti.
Somigliavo ad una nave
d'argento scalza
pronta a pescare al fondo
le lucciole e gli amori.
Erano bianche le mie impronte
tra i tramonti,
come l'onda trascorsa a
ritornare bagliore.

As a Venus

It seemed to me silent, the night
in a caress dark of moments.
His arms gathered me up
out of the perfume of the day
and they led me into a ground
that spied the dreams and the clouds.
The angel's glances,
they desired my breath
in order to incite distant hearts extinguished
and masked tears of joy.
I put on the light
and I let go of myself to dip among the branches
and the wheat.
I sang in choir hymns to life
among the swarming of pollens
and resins.
I made the sky love me
as a Venus clinging
to the winds.
I was compared to a silver barefoot ship
ready to fish from the deep
fireflies and romances.
They were white, my imprints
among sunsets,
as a wave passed to
returning shine.

Cromosoma libero

Non faccio che pensare a te.
Pur di averti qui
t'immagino tra le nuvole,
sei lo sfondo azzurro dei miei giorni,
ti creo con lo sguardo,
ogni volta che fisso il cielo
appari allo specchio dell'alba.
Hai le guance di sole,
bruci la terra per avvicinarti a me.
Ti sento respirare
nelle melodie dei gabbiani,
cammini sulle acque
in equilibrio sulle vibrazioni
della sabbia calda.
Travolgi gli orizzonti,
nasci dentro i tramonti,
sconfini oltre i monti,
hai mille distanze.
Dondoli tra le ore
negli orologi delle stagioni,
sei ovunque
io t'accompagno.
Sali sulle mie mani
minuscola cellula
d'emozione,
ti svegli quando il cuore
bussa alla città,
cromosoma libero
dentro me.

Free Chromosome

I do not think of you.
Only in order to have you here
I imagine you among the clouds,
you are the azure background of my days,
I make you with the glance,
each time that I stare at the sky
you appear as the mirror of the dawn.
You have cheeks of sun,
you burn the earth for bringing you near to me.
I feel you breathing
in the melodies of the seagulls,
you walk on water
in balance on the vibrations
of the warm sand.
You overwhelm horizons,
you begin inside sunsets,
you trespass beyond mountains,
you have a thousand distances.
You oscillate between the times,
in the clockwork of the seasons,
you are everywhere
I follow you.
You climb onto my hands
diminutive cells
of emotions,
you wake when the heart
knocks at the city,
free chromosome
inside me.

E restiamo come vele

Davanti a noi il cielo accantona
nuvole e lontananza,
soli di ghiaccio e panni rossi.
La vita è lì
che ci scorre negli occhi
e nelle vene
tra grossi dubbi e silenzi.
Suonano i passi
delle rughe che scrivono
il tempo dentro e fuori
le carni.
Ci avvolge la notte,
la furia del giorno
una terra materna
ed un mare che sfila sussurri
dondolante.
E restiamo come vele
ad aspettare che si spogli
un sorriso all'orizzonte.

And We Remain Like Sails

In front of us the sky sets aside
clouds and distance,
only of ice and red linens.
The life is there
that passes us in the eyes
and in the veins
between huge doubts and silences.
They sound the steps
in the wrinkles that they write
the time inside and outside
the flesh.
It winds up the night for us,
the fury of the day
a maternal earth
and a sea that extracts oscillating
whispers.
And we remain like sails
waiting when a smile undresses
on the horizon.

Fango e radici

Affoghiamo le nostre miserie
con le lacrime.
Siamo spiriti di un secolo
che divora le memorie.
Giochiamo con il destino
come fosse una palla
da infilare nella rete.
Cerchiamo il guidizio
di Dio,
la Sua voce affascinante
per una rivelazione
di vita eterna.
L'amore è la pioggia
che non aspettiamo.
Accettiamo il dolore
e ci completiamo
col sollievo di altri.
Ci vediamo acque
di mari diversi,
figli di burrasca.
Ci incontriamo
nel petto della stessa terra,
fango e radici
per un nuovo germoglio.

Mud and Roots

We smother our miseries
with tears.
We are spirits of an age
that devours memories.
We play with destiny
like it was a ball
to put in the net.
We seek the judgment
of God,
Her fascinating voice
for a revelation
of eternal life.
Love is the rain
that we do not expect.
We accept sorrow
and we carry ourselves through
with the reliefs of others.
We see ourselves waters
of several seas,
children of storms.
We meet
in the bosom of the same earth,
mud and roots
for a new sprout.

Padre

Padre,
mi vanto del colore e del suono
che ridendo rincorri
per stagioni e grembi di luce.
Dico alla pelle
quanto entrambi affondiamo radici
in estro e città.
Occupi sempre più
il profondo del mio giocare alla vita,
quello spazio di somiglianza calda
alle vetrine di un sogno.
In parte nel tuo asfalto di uomo
cerco vapori d'eterno orgoglio,
quel silenzio che so
veliero di grande calore.

Father

Father,
I boast of the color and of the sound
that, laughing, you pursue
across seasons and wombs of light.
I say to the skin
how much we both sink roots
into impulse and cities.
You always occupy more
depth of my playing at life,
that space of warm similarity
to the glass cabinets of a dream.
In part, in your asphalt of man
I seek vapors of everlasting pride,
that silence that I know,
sailing ship of great warmth.

Madre

Nasco da te
inclusa in un singhiozzo di vita
ed il tuo inondar di bene
si rifà alla vendemmia di una luce
che è impegno con l'amore
e con la fede.
Non so se riesco a darti orgoglio
del mio intimo ed elegante privilegio
d'esistere.
In questa anima che è terra anche tua
provo a tenere il cielo
e quelle fragilità ereditarie al tuo sangue.
I miei occhi sono come grappoli d'istante
sempre fradici d'affetto,
sorridono
e vanno a farsi specchio
nel tuo materno splendore.

Mother

I'm born from you
enclosed in a hiccup of life
and your flood of good
it repeats at the harvest of a light
which is commitment with love
and with faith.
I do not know whether I succeed at giving you pride
of my innermost and the elegant privilege
of existing.
In this spirit that is territory also yours
I try to hold heaven
and those fragilities hereditary to your blood.
My eyes are as clusters of moments
always soaked in fondness,
they smile
and they work to mirror
your maternal splendor.

Ad una padova leggera

Occhi d'una città
tanto fine e ritrovata,
vi ascolto nel batticuore d'una vita
animata di radici e ricordi
senza pudore.

C'è come un puro amore
ad una Padova leggera e adolescente
in questo mio clamore
di battiti e respiri.

Subito vivo, sparsa sulle piazze,
nelle ombre di raffinati marciapiedi
e semafori.

La mia presenza sembra
muta timidezza alle nuvole,
precoce fantasia che trema limpida
l'origine.

Vengo tra gli amici
e tra gli adulti sentieri
a partorire lo spirito di una terra
tanto cara e coetanea.

Nel bianco odore dell'aria,
dentro la rugiada che è mia,
ardo d'emozioni antiche.

To a Fickle Padua

Eyes of a city
so fine and found,
I listen to you all in the palpitations of a life
animated by roots and memories
without modesty.

It is like a pure love
to a fickle and adolescent Padua
in this my clamor
of heartbeats and breaths.

Immediately alive, scattered on the square,
in the shadows of refined sidewalks
and traffic lights.

My presence seems
mute shyness to the clouds,
premature fantasy that shivers limpid
origins.

I come between friends
and between adult pathways
to bring forth the spirit of a place
so dear and contemporary.

In the clean smell of the air,
inside the dew that is mine,
I burn with ancient emotions.

Al tempio del destino

Una sagoma di luce e silenzio
mi porta a spingere aria e vene in cielo.
Non invecchia la mia fede
e durante una pioggia di fiato
suono a Dio l'urto beato delle nuvole,
affidando snelle purezze
a quelle superfici di donna
che a natura assomigliano in fretta.
Sento nevicate di preghiere
e resurrezioni
al solo nutrire il midollo d'orizzonti.
Con le narici aperte al verde
della vita,
con gli occhi odore del mare
invito la mia fragilità ad affacciarsi
al tempio del destino.
E rinasco in alba un pò meno carne,
e mi faccio terra, ramo o sogno
per amore.

To the Temple of Fate

An outline of light and silence
moves me to drive air and veins to heaven.
It doesn't age, my faith,
and during a lasting rain of breath
I play to God the happy collision of clouds,
trusting slender purities
to that one surface of woman
that to nature they resemble in briskness.
I feel snowfalls of prayers
and resurrections
to the only feeding, the marrow of horizons.
With nostrils open to the green
of life,
with eyes that smell of the sea
I invite my fragility to show itself
to the temple of destiny.
And I am born again in dawn a bit less flesh,
and I make myself earth, branch, or dream
for love.

Aria d'ottobre

Mi specchio in pupille di quercia
e sento l'autunno impazzire di rossore
tra tende di linfe adolescenti.
La mia pelle si aggrappa
a cascate di rugiada,
scopre fiumi di giallo alle origini.
Mi stringo al grappolo legnoso,
religioso ormeggio
alla vita.
Una foglia cade.
Ed io, aria d'ottobre
m'inchino a bere elemosine di terra.

Aria of October

I see myself in pupils of oak
and I feel autumn going crazy in blush
in between curtains of adolescent saps.
My skin clings to herself
to waterfalls of dew,
it sweeps rivers of yellow to the origins.
I shrink to a dry cluster,
religious mooring
to life.
A sheet falls.
And I, aria of October,
I bow myself to drink alms of earth.

Che stagione ho tra le dita?

Che stagione ho tra le dita?
Non è il solito autunno
che piange rossore.
Non si spiega questo ottobre
che mi fa cenni d'aria d'estate.
Inesperta alla volontà del tempo
strofino la mia voce
in un nudo giallo di foglia,
accanto a gioconde polveri di cielo.
Mi piace ingombrare le ciglia
di scialli di rugiade,
mi piace invocare albe fanciulle.
In un ritornello d'alberi e strade,
come per amore
tremo calore
e torno grappolo di sogno.

Which Season Do I Have Between My Fingers?

Which season do I have between my fingers?
It is not the usual autumn
that rains redness.
It doesn't become clear this October
which gestures to me with summer air.
Inexperienced to the will of time
I move my voice
in a naked layer of yellow,
next to light-hearted dusts from the sky.
It pleases me to encumber the eyelashes
with shawls of dews,
it pleases me to invoke young dawns.
In a refrain of trees and roads,
as for love
I shiver warmth
and I return cluster of dream.

La mia terra sott'acqua

Nella retina il bruciore
di un precipizio liquido,
la mia terra sott'acqua.
Dal cielo gerarchie di pioggia
rantolano dentro zolle gonfie
e scalze.
Sequenze di tuono
e spighe invecchiate
sembrano in guerra ad altra nazione
di mare.
Come odora di disperazione
il fango che spia nocche e lacrime
di paesi rimasti senza forma
e colore.
Mi sforzo a divorare in memoria
l'ordine affettuoso di perfette pianure,
il pudore di betulle e pascoli felici.
Qualcuno in un girotondo
di sordi detriti e pallidi vigneti
riassume l'inferno
sotto i piedi.

My Underwater Land

In the retina the burning
of a liquid precipice,
my ground underwater.
From the sky hierarchies of rain
gasp inside swollen clods
and barefoot.
Sequences of thunder
and aged grain
seem at war with another
sea nation.
Like the smell of despair,
mud that spies knuckles and tears
of countries, you remained without form
and color.
I labor to devour in memory
the affectionate order of perfect plains,
the modesty of birches and happy pastures.
Somebody in a spin
of dull rubble and pallid vineyards
resumes the hell
below the feet.

Le solitudini

(Poesia tratta da un'opera di Vittorio Pavoncello)

Ombre astratte
crescono inverni negli occhi.
Trasloco lacrime
in un tappeto di ciglia e macerie.
Vengono in vertebra
pollini e ritmi di tenebra.
Rotolano il tempo
le solitudini,
mi legano indecenti
ad una pelle in fuga.
Schiacciata dalla prepotenza
di un nudo silenzio,
riempio il fiato di burrasca
e mozziconi di vuoto.
Come ghiaccio nero
sfoglio i miei abissi
e pettino l'iride
di attese di luce.

The Loneliness(es)
(a poem taken from an opera by Vittorio Pavoncello)

Shadows abstracted
they grow winters in the eyes.
I move tears
on a mat of eyelashes and ruins.
They come in vertebra
pollens and rhythms of obscurity.
They spin time,
the lonelinesses,
They bind me indecently
to a skin in flight.
Crushing from the force
of a bare silence,
I fill the breath of hostility
and stumps of emptiness.
Like black ice
I tear off my abysses
and I scold the iris
for expectations of light.

Parentesi di lontananza

Padova,
mi compare
il dominio delle tue nebbie
in gola
ed ogni tanto tremo parentesi
di lontananza.
Immersa in un verbo di pianura
riempio memorie
di fronti di vigneto ed arterie di resina.
Scolpito in seno
ho suono di vendemmie,
il rincorrersi lucido di rugiade.
È solo un misero addio
a dividermi dal ritmo delle origini.
Intatto il grano,
sa le mie lacrime.

Parentheses of Distance

Padua,
the dominion of your fogs
appears
in the throat
and every so often I shiver parentheses
of distance.
Immersed in a verb of level ground
I fill memories
of vineyard fronts and arteries of resin.
Imprinted in the breast
I have the sound of grape harvests,
the chasing polish of dews.
It is only a miserable goodbye
to divide me from the rhythm of the origins.
Untouched, the grain
knows my tears.

Nel domani

Nel domani
incarto la fragranza dei miei silenzi,
graffio dal cielo la luce
che mi sfida a dirigere
stagioni e miniature
di secoli.
Imploro gli occhi
di non affogare
in fili di sagome e promesse.
Ho bisogno
di un sogno,
di un inchino alla luna,
di un senso da offrire
al seno del mondo.
Nel marciare
di vene e destino,
mi vedo gioco d'acque,
suono di fuoco,
cometa d'aria,
vibrazione di terra.
E stabile nuvola
lascio la pelle
a ripassare
l'odore della vita.

In the Future

In the future
I wrap the fragrance of my silences,
I scratch the light from the sky
that dares me to direct
seasons and miniatures
of centuries.
I implore the eyes
to not drown
in filaments of outlines and promises.
I need
a dream,
a curtsy to the moon,
a sense of offering
to the breast of the world.
In the working
of blood vessels and fate,
I see myself playing in water,
the sound of fire,
comet of air,
vibration of earth.
And steady cloud
I let the skin go
to come by again
the smell of life.

Scartafacci di vita
(a Pier Paolo Pasolini)

Nelle fragilità del tempo,
tra miserabili scartafacci di vita
è ancora umano
amalgamare parole e coraggio
al costato
di un glicine e ad obliqui occhi
di città.
Pier Paolo, patimento oscuro
è dentro le vestali del tuo quartiere
e nel ciclo di pietre assorte
a diventare silenzio.
Tradito come un autunno
in maledizione
è stato il tuo canto di verità.
Non si accorsero che assassinando
un guscio secolare di saggezza
estirpavano fiore universale di poesia.

Life's Scibblings / Blatherings
(to Pier Paolo Pasolini)

In the fragilities of the time,
among miserable scribblings of life
it is still human
to amalgamate words and courage
to the ribs
of a wisteria and to oblique eyes
of the city.
Pier Paolo, dark suffering
is inside the vestals of your quarters
and in the cycle of stones absorbed
with becoming silence.
Betrayed as an autumn
in damnation
it was your song of truth.
They did not realize that assassinating
a shell centuries old with wisdom
they eradicated the universal bloom of poetry.

Veggenze

Letture scomposte
nella polvere.
La mia anima fruga
nel rovescio del mondo,
messaggi sublimi,
impalpabili.
Nascono fili
di luce improvvisa.
Rabbrividisco.
Nitide veggenze,
nude apparenze mai scoperte
scelgono altri sensi.
Perpetue mosse già
pronte ad esistere
e crescere dentro alla fune
di un pensiero,
cedono il passo
ad un fugace incontro
di misteri.
Non posso fingere.
Oltre di me,
niente ha sensi eguali.
Cambio il sistema
sbriciolo immagini
e creo fiamme gelide
col potere del nulla.

Clairvoyance

Readings unseemly
in the dust.
My soul rummages
in the insides of the world,
sublime messages,
impalpable.
They are born wires
of sudden light.
I shiver.
Clear clairvoyance,
naked appearances never exposed
they choose other meanings.
Perpetual motion by now
ready to exist
and to grow inside a line
of a thought,
they give up the passage
to a fleeting encounter
of mysteries.
I cannot imagine.
Beyond me,
nothing has felt equal.
I change the system
I crumble images
and I make freezing flames
with the ability of nothing.

Dei tuoi Navigli
(ad Alda Merini)

Era bacio maledetto
quell'arteria di luce
chiusa nelle ultime saggezze
di novembre.
Quello sguardo ingordo di poesia
svaniva dietro impulsi astratti
d'autunno.
La morte molestò il suono
dei tuoi Navigli,
sconvolse il verde dei tuoi respiri.
Alda, io in te cerco radice ai miei silenzi,
sogno riparo ad un equivoco di solitudini.
Intorno a una grandezza di ciglia
e orizzonti,
i miei umili spiragli d'istinto scapigliato
come intoccabili destini
alla tua memoria concedo.

Of Your Canals
(to Alda Merini)

The kiss was damned
that artery of light
shut in the final wisdoms
of November.
That glance greedy for poetry
disappeared behind abstracted impulses
of autumn.
The death harassed the sound
of your canals,
it upset the green of your breaths.
Alda, I search in you for roots to my silences,
dream fixed to a misunderstanding of solitudes.
Around a bulk of eyelashes
and horizons,
my modest glimmerings of disheveled intuition
like untouchable fates
to your memory I concede.

Un fraterno silenzio (a Federico)

Io so di un fraterno silenzio,
una miniatura di esistenze
che ci accomuna nel fiato e nelle ciglia.
Ritrovo in uno sguardo
un nido di sogni
e quel cancello di sangue
simile per dolcezza
a stanze di madre e di padre.
Mi rallegra la rossa stagione
in cui ti fai uomo
aperto al mondo e al suo odore.
Incarnato come un orizzonte
sui prati delle mie impronte
stai come un figlio
a cercare soggiorno nel mio coraggio.
Ed io fiera di essere invasa
dalla tua somiglianza,
faccio ritorno al porto
di un maturo affetto.

A Brotherly Silence (to Federico)

I know of a brotherly silence,
a miniature of existence
that joins us in the breath and in the eyelashes.
I find in a glance
a nest of dreams
and that gate of blood
akin to sweetness
to rooms of mother and of father.
It makes me happy the red season
in which you become man
open to the world and to its smell.
Incarnate as a horizon
on the fields of my signs
you remain like a son
seeking a sojourn in my courage.
And I, proud of being invaded
by your likeness,
I return to the port
of a mature affection.

Così t'amo

Così t'amo
in un mutamento di cielo,
in un modesto respiro
fatto di pascoli e fiume.
Mi completo
come l'albero al suo fusto
in un intreccio di sensi maturi.
Della tua argilla di uomo
mi nutro
ed in fronte
porto la forma di un beneficio
di rossori.
Assolta nell'azzurro
di un tuo sguardo
vado ad immergere l'anima
in un palmo sincero di luce.
E allineando le emozioni
in un bacio,
ripeto all'universo
l'umano colore
di un equilibrio raggiunto,
ripeto al destino
l'amore e le tue sembianze.

As I Love You

As I love you
in a change of the sky,
in a modest breath
made of pastures and rivers.
I complete myself
as a tree to its trunk
in a twist of mature feelings.
From your clay of being
I feed myself
and on my forehead
I carry the appearance of a growth
of redness.
Absolved in the azure
of one of your looks
I go to immerse the soul
in an honest span of light.
And aligning the emotions
in a kiss,
I repeat to the universe
the human color
of a balance reached,
I repeat to destiny
the love and your features.

Eternità di rossore

Tu mi hai riempito di vita,
come un'alba
che si sente madre
in una zolla di luce.
Così l'amore vive
della comunione di cieli
e sostanze,
unghie e orizzonti.
Con il solo respiro
delle tue ciglia,
io rinnovo il clima
delle mie carni,
apro i sensi
a spettacoli d'oceano.
Affamata d'onde e di paradisi,
ti parlo di una sorte
che fa di noi
eternità di rossore,
colore nudo di scogli.

Eternity of Blush

You have filled me with life,
like a dawn
that feels maternal
in a clump of light.
In this way love lives
in a communion of heavens
and substances,
nails and horizons.
With the lone breath
of your eyelashes,
I renew the climate
of my flesh,
I open the senses
to sights of ocean.
Starved of waves and of paradises,
I speak to you of a fate
that makes us
eternity of blush,
color bare of cliffs.

L'acqua ed il pane di un riseveglio

L'acqua ed il pane di un risveglio
e di nuovo appare una febbre di linfe,
voce o luce d'infusi azzurri,
un cielo
in rami a gocce
a reggere naturali meditazioni.
Avviene in vena
tempo di primavere,
un fiato acceso e lucido di collina.
La mia pelle intende
l'acqua ed il pane di un risveglio,
come petali fanciulli
a contemplare
echi di rossore ancora verde.

The Water and the Bread of an Awakening

The water and the bread of an awakening
and it appears again a fever of sap,
voice or light of blue infusions,
a sky
in branches to drops
to withstanding natural meditations.
It happens in vein,
season of springtimes,
a glowing breath and hill's shine.
My skin understands
the water and the bread of an awakening,
like childish petals
contemplating
echoes of blush still unripe.

Da un amore

Da un amore
che ritaglia docili fiati di luce
ho appreso che un brivido
prepara stanze calde
dentro i secoli.
Mi sorprende il rumore
di sguardi lontani,
il gesto di un vapore nudo
che si mostra faro in viali di resina.
Dalle grate di un'assenza
strappo periferie di voci,
cemento attorcigliato all'anima.
Credo
di rompere in temporale
le mie solitudini.
L'abitudine al tuo calore
mi fa deglutire instabili orizzonti.
Contando ogni filare di nuvola
attendo.
E sulla mia bocca conservo
azzurri necessari.

From a Love

From a love
that cuts out docile breaths of light
I have learned that a shiver
prepares warm rooms
within centuries.
It surprises me, the sound
of faraway glances,
the gesture of a naked vapor
which shows itself beacon in boulevards of resin.
From the grating of an absence
I pull out peripheries of voices,
cement twisted to the soul.
I believe
in breaking in time
my lonelinesses.
The routine to your heat
makes me swallow changing horizons.
Counting each line of cloud
I await.
And on my mouth I preserve
necessary azures.

Inguini di memoria

Inguini di memoria
adagio sul grembo
di una terra d'ambra,
dove è nata la mia prima fame
di confine.
In un tremore di resina
stringo la certezza
di una zolla assente,
catturo la vendemmia fredda
di asfalti silenziosi.
Come un'offerta di luce
la mia vita
si misura nel vuoto dell'erba,
tra parentesi di linfa bambina.
Ho gustato l'origine
in tendini di foglia,
dentro il volto
di un sentiero che è paese
e carne devota
a forze di cielo.
Della pianura
la mia sorte
protegge gli embrioni
di un umido orizzonte
che chiama.
E mi fa ritornare.

Groins of Memory

Groins of memory
I lay down gently on the womb
of an amber earth
where my first hunger was born
from confines.
In a tremor of resin
I squeeze the certainty
of an absent clump,
I capture the cold harvest
of hushed asphalts.
Like an offering of light
my life
measures itself in the nothingness of grass
between parentheses of young sap.
I have tasted the origin
in tendons of leaves,
inside the essence
of a way that is country
and devoted flesh
to forces of heaven.
From the plain
my destiny
protects the embryos
of a damp future
that calls.
And it makes me return.

Imparo l'amore

Imparo l'amore
dal gergo dei tuoi occhi,
come fossero aria e giusta dimora.
Dove le tue pupille
sono pronte
a sfamare
il popolo dei miei silenzi,
io vedo il colore della vita,
la docile acqua del destino.
Le tue ciglia
sanno formare l'onda,
le tue ciglia
sanno suonare tremori
alla mia terra segreta.

I Learn Love

I learn love
from the jargon of your eyes
like they were air and decent abode.
Where your pupils
are ready
to care for
the crowd of my silences,
I see the color of life,
the docile water of fate.
Your eyelashes
can form the wave,
your eyelashes
can ring tremors
to my secret ground.

Lasciami il calore paziente

Lasciami il calore paziente
delle tue ciglia,
ho capito che dentro i tuoi occhi
salvo il mio destino.
L'amore lo tengo tra i polsi
e le tue labbra,
nelle briciole chiare
di un familiare vapore.
Mi hanno raccolto
celesti sfere,
l'albero e la corteccia
di un suono maschile.
La mia vita matura
accanto alle tue acque.
La mia vita conosce in te
il mare e l'assoluto.

Leave me the Patient Warmth

Leave me the patient warmth
of your eyelashes,
I understood that within your eyes
I preserve my fate.
The love I hold between the pulses
and your lips,
in the clear crumbs
of a familiar vapor.
They have gathered me,
heavenly spheres,
the tree and the bark
of a masculine sound.
My life matures
next to your waters.
My life experiences in you
the sea and the absolute.

Mediterraneo
(poesia ispirata alle musiche di Gianni Gandi)

Acque materne battezzano
catene di scogli,
il sole ha radunato il suono
di nudi sensi di luce in schiuma.
In un viaggio di ciglia
Il Mediterraneo si mescola
alle mie narici,
scioglie il suo azzurro
dietro solstizi di solitudine.
Il mare raccoglie preghiere
dai fondali,
sazia di meraviglia l'inferno
di zolle indurite dalle croci.
Sulla sabbia rimbalzano eternità,
chiome di mandorli e conchiglie assetate.
Il bianco dell'aria
si riempie alla foce
di fiati di musica.

Mediterranean
(poem inspired by the music of Gianni Gandi)

Maternal waters christen
ranges of cliff,
the sun has gathered the sound
of nude senses of light in froth.
In a journey of eyelashes
the Mediterranean blends
in my nostrils,
it unleashes its azure
behind solstices of solitudes.
The sea gathers prayers
from its bottom,
satiates hell with marvel
of clumps hardened by the crosses.
On the sand they bounce off eternity,
foliage of almond trees and thirsty shells.
The white of the air
fills the mouth of the river
with breaths of music.

Nel bianco della vita

Il mondo lo cerco
nel lievito di un cielo primitivo,
al centro di una scintilla
non umana,
nel pudore di colori adolescenti.
E so che il gergo del tempo
non muta il mio costante scrutare
solchi e respiri di terra.
Provo il fascino
di una rugiada perfetta,
m'infilo nel bianco della vita,
lavo le mie carni
in embrioni di religione
ed apro il palato
ad un avvenire
che mi chiama.

In the White of Life

The world I look for
in the yeast of a primitive sky,
at the center of a spark
not human,
in the shyness of adolescent colors.
And I know that the jargon of the time
doesn't change my constant scrutinizing
of the grooves and breaths of earth.
I experience the fascination
of a perfect dew,
I slip into the white of life,
I clean my flesh
in embryos of religion
and I open the palate
to a future
that calls me.

Nelle tiepide ombre del tempo

La terra attende il ritorno
di stagioni perfette
e ragioni complici
di civile memoria.
Il clima cambia'
al tocco di fiati
e smarrimenti segreti.
Il suono fraterno
di fiumi e nuvole
si adagia nel solco
di equilibri dispersi.
Avido è il destino
che strappa
muscolature di confine
alla luna e al misero uomo.
Nelle tiepide ombre del tempo
un mutamento di suolo
chiude il cielo e l'orrizonte
in un gergo turchese
di liquide solitudini.
Si vive
tra ghiaccio e aridità
nell'utero muto
di un uiverso senza sguardo.

In the Tepid Shadows of the Time

The ground awaits the return
of perfect seasons
and complicit reasons
of civil memory.
The climate changes
to the touch of breath
and secret confusions.
The brotherly sound
of rivers and clouds
reclines in the furrow
of dispersed equilibriums.
Greedy is the fate
that tears
musculature from boundaries
to the moon and to the miserable man.
In the tepid shadows of the time
a change from the ground
closes the sky and the horizon
in a turquoise jargon
of fluid loneliness.
We live
between ice and aridity
in the mute uterus
of a universe without view.

Quest'epoca disarma

Quest'epoca disarma
i germogli del domani,
risucchia i colori
di semplici umanità,
preme i giorni al deserto.
In un ronzio di croci
non mancano
nervose abbondanze
di miseria,
il rapido maturare
di precipizi all'anima.
Per rimuovere il fremito del crollo,
agli uomini è concesso
attingere alle vene di Dio,
agli uomini è concesso
sfamarsi al tremore di un sangue
stretto in recinti
di grazia eterna.

This Epoch Disarms

This epoch disarms
the buds of the future,
engulfs the colors
of basic humanity,
presses the days to the desert.
In a whir of crosses
not lacking
nervous abundance
of misery,
the rapid maturing
of downfalls of the soul.
In order to remove the trembling of the fall,
it was granted to the men
drawing to the veins of God,
it was granted to the men
caring for the tremor of a blood
tight in enclosures
of eternal grace.

Segrete metamorfosi

Il mio sangue vive
segrete metamorfosi,
affolla il destino
di calore ed inganni.
Alle dita ho appeso
la certezza di una luce
assetata di vita,
alle caviglie porto l'edera
di follie macchiate
di confine.
Uno schianto di polveri e grano
confessa origini da sfamare,
solleva carità di macerie familiari.
Tornano in pupilla ricordi,
percezioni di nebbia,
grigi deliri.
Nel respiro fragile di un fiume
rincorro la mia ombra.
E trovo timide assenze,
una luna di vento.

Secret Metamorphoses

My blood lives
secret metamorphoses,
it crowds fate
with heat and tricks.
At the fingers I have hung
the certainty of a light
thirsty for life,
to the ankles I bring the ivy
of follies stained
by boundaries.
One crash of dust and wheat
confesses origins from feeding,
it lifts charity from familiar ruins.
They return in the pupil, memories,
perceptions of fog,
grey delusions.
In the frail breath of a river
I run after my shadow.
And I find shy absences,
a moon of wind.

Sono spogli i Navigli
(ad Alda Merini)

Sono spogli i Navigli,
non hanno più rughe di poesia
da vegliare,
non hanno più pupille
assetate d'amore
da proteggere.
La polvere conserva la fragranza
di silenzi intessuti di cielo.
Sul dorso di una strada
impronte di rime
tornano a bere
sorsi di volontà,
fiati di sillabe
tornano a baciare dimensioni
con lo sguardo benevolo
di una donna,
che educa la sua anima
a restare alba
devota alla terra.

The Canals are Bare
(to Alda Merini)

The canals are bare,
they don't have any more wrinkles of poetry
to keep watch over,
they don't have any more pupils
thirsty of love
from protecting.
The dust preserves the aroma
of silences woven together by the sky.
On the back of a road,
imprints of rhymes
they go back to drinking
sips of will,
breaths of syllables,
they go back to kissing dimensions
with the benevolent look
of a woman,
who teaches her soul
to remain dawn
devoted to the earth.

Poi, il silenzio

Sappiamo di una sorte
che sembra stagione che persiste,
un ripetersi divino ed antico,
un rintracciare ombre
nel volto della vita.
Il colore che si attende
è sui muscoli di un sogno.
Dentro la luna
altri mondi, un rumore d'acque scolpite.
Poi, il silenzio.

Then, Silence

We know of a destiny
that seems a season that persists,
a repeating, divine and ancient,
a shadow tracking down
in the face of life.
The expected color
is on the muscles of a dream.
Inside the moon
other worlds, a sound of sculpted waters.
Then, the silence.

Come alberi

Si sono ammucchiati
secoli
come alberi
in questo mondo
che sa di risse
e di ossa spalancate.
La mia sagoma insiste
ad allontanare smarrimenti
in un cielo che muore.
E sottile si fa vergogna
del sangue che si ripete.

Like Trees

They accumulated
centuries
like trees
in this world
which knows of scuffles
and of bones thrust open.
My outline persists
at expelling confusion
in a sky that dies.
And faint, it feels ashamed
of the blood that repeats itself.

Parabole materne

Non credere che un roco confine
possa alterare le tonalità
di un affetto.
La mia carne ha premura
delle tue stagioni
e crede ancora nella pienezza
delle tue parabole materne.
Annusando la superficie
di un silenzio
vedo quella dolcezza di grano
che si sacrifica eterna
al mio addio.

Maternal Parables

Do not believe that a hoarse boundary
can alter the shades
of an affection.
My flesh has the consideration
of your seasons
and still believes in the fullness
of your maternal parables.
Smelling the surfaces
of a silence
I see that sweetness of wheat
which offers itself everlasting
to my farewell.

Non chiedo molto

Mi rimangono un sogno
ed una bianca devozione
all'attesa.
Tendo la mente
all'eco di altri cieli.
Non chiedo molto.
Solo un seguace
del mio pesante rincorrermi

I Don't Ask For Much

They remain to me a dream
and a white devotion
to the awaited.
I stretch the mind
to the echo of other skies.
I don't ask for much.
Only a follower
of my heavy pursuing me.

Una patria sospesa

Sono rimasta in quest'alba di memorie
aggrappata a sottili fili di luce,
sciacquandomi la pelle in un silenzio.
Ricordo il cielo
a nidificare tra stagioni
ed alveari d'infinito.
Avvolta nel ventre di una nuvola,
mescolata al bianco di un orizzonte
ho toccato un sogno,
il colore buono
di una patria sospesa.

A Homeland Suspended

I stayed in this dawn of memories
clung to thin wires of light,
washing my skin in a silence.
I remember the sky
nesting between seasons
and infinite beehives.
Wound in the womb of a cloud,
mixed into the white of a horizon
I touched a dream,
the good color
of a homeland suspended.

Orizzonte antico (dal fontanone al Gianicolo)

In un incendio d'acque
spruzzi di pietra,
la grazia di un verde altissimo.
M'accoglie il drago che si nutre
senza canto di secoli ingordi,
sollevando alle ciglia
veloci e liquide trasparenze.
Il sudore di un orizzonte antico
scrive che la mia volontà
è schiena di un glicine
spento in velluti pasoliniani.
La vita mi ha portato
il galoppo di sillabe e stelle romane,
il lampo di visioni andate in gola.
Verso un'estate che rumoreggia
lievi confessioni
scavo sovranità di solitudine
e mi porto alle dita la saggezza
di un civile silenzio,
che in abiti d'olmo, di platano e d'eroismi perduti,
difende tutta la mia ingenuità.

Ancient Horizon (at the Gianicolo Fountain)

In a blaze of waters
splashes of rock,
the grace of a highest green.
He welcomes me, the dragon that feeds
without song of greedy centuries,
lifting to the eyelashes
quick and liquid transparencies.
The sweat of an ancient horizon
writes that my will
is the spine of a lifeless wisteria
smooth Pasolinian.
The life that I have worn
the gallop of syllables and Roman stars,
the lightning of visions gone in throat.
I experience a summer that rumbles
soft confessions
I reveal sovereignties of solitude
and I bring myself to the fingers the wisdom
of a civil silence,
that in the attire of an elm, of a sycamore, and of lost heroisms,
it protects all my naivety.

Italia

Questa terra indossa
alfabeti di luci antiche.
Il suono dei suoi colori
ha schiene di memorie
intatte al cielo,
campanili,
destini di pianura
a riempire cime
in espressioni di mare.
Sui fianchi
sorde frontiere,
solchi di distanze
nel riflesso della sorte.
Ogni pozzanghera, polvere o ramo
è umore che genera amore all'origine.
Io che di patria parlo
come di una verde madre,
rivolta a bianche malinconie di nebbia,
infrango limiti rossi di linfa
e respiro
energia dalla storia,
dalle cicatrici di un tempo
che è ombra di un tricolore,
orgoglio a ciglia di mondo.

Italy

This land wears
alphabets of antique lights.
The sound of her colors
has spines of memories
intact to heaven,
belfries,
destinies of level ground
filling peaks
in manifestations of sea.
On the sides
deaf borders,
ruts of distances
in the reflex of fate.
Each puddle, dust or branch
is temperament that provokes love for the origins.
I speak of homeland
as of a green mother,
she revolts against whites melancholies of fog,
I break red edges of sap
and inhale
energy from the past
from scars of a time
that is shade of the flag,
pride on the world's eyelashes.

Giovanni Paolo II

Le mie giovani guance,
a piedi nudi tra le stagioni
ricordano la radiosità beata
del tuo fiato.
Avverto la tua tunica bianca
ancora in ginocchio al mondo
e mille occhi ad offrirti gratitudine.
Si mescolano al cielo
preghiere e fragranze di eternità.
In sacre forme di vita,
dalle luci calde e distese
si avvera un polline,
un nome di uomo e di padre
che per non svanire
ha colore di mare e di confine.
So ritrovarti
segreto nel mio sangue
ad ogni pausa di silenzio,
come sull'alba che docile
fruga tra i miracoli.

Giovanni Paolo II

My young cheeks,
on bare feet across the seasons,
they remember the happy radiance
of your breath.
I feel your white tunic
still in the knees of the world
and one thousand eyes offering you gratitude.
They merge in the sky
prayers and fragrances of eternity.
In sacred conventions of life,
from the warm lights and expanses
a pollen becomes reality,
a man's name and a father's
which, in order to not vanish,
has color of sea and of limits.
I know how to find you
secret in my blood
to each pause of silence
as the dawn, which docile,
rummages through miracles.

Monteverde e le mie guance

Puntuali gli olmi
di via Ozanam
spalancano ruggine verde
addosso ad altezze di palazzi
e cellule di passanti.
Paziente il mio fiato
s'infila tra gerarchie antiche
di marciapiedi,
nel raffinato vapore
d'un orgoglio selvaggio
che fu vertice di poesia
e vita
in sangue a Pasolini.
Ad un bivio,
Monteverde e le mie guance
ereditano silenzi
dalle confessioni randagie
di un pino.
Soffi di preghiera,
frammenti di santità
educano scalini
e nocche di terrazze
al pesante calore di storia.
L'essere nei miei occhi
a riprodurre rossori di glicine
e criniere di pietra
maschera lucidità d'origini
lontane.

Monteverde and My Cheeks

The prompt elm trees
of Ozanam road
they open wide green resentments
on top of the heights of buildings
and cells of pedestrians.
Patient my breath
slips in between ancient hierarchies
of sidewalks,
in the refined vapor
of a primitive hubris
that was the summit of poetry
and life
in blood to Pasolini.
At a crossroads,
Monteverde and my cheeks
inherit silences
from the confessions
of a pine.
Breaths of prayer,
fragments of sanctity
they teach steps
and knuckles on terraces
the weighted heat of history.
It being in my eyes
to reproduce blushes of wisteria
and manes of rock
mask lucidity of origins
distant.

Il trionfo del dramma

Il terrore scoppia
come brusio e confessione
di silenzi
alle palpebre.
Pessimo è il suo colore
negli archivi di midolli innocenti.
Rischiano l'urlo, il trionfo del dramma
talloni d'ebrei vene incarnate in carbone
e gusci di fiato senza riposo.
Si schiantano mani e righe di schegge.
All'orizzonte larve di polvere
cercano il tessuto
del rimanere memoria.

The Triumph of the Drama

The terror explodes
as bustle and confession
of silences
by the eyelids.
Its color is terrible
in the archives of innocent marrows.
They endanger the shout, the triumph of the drama
heels of Jews, veins embodied in coal
and shells of breath without rest.
Hands crash and stripes of lightning.
At the horizon wrecks of dust
search for the fabric
of the remaining memory.

Gioco d'identità

Gioco d'identità
in un palmo di voce maschile,
il movimento interiore
di uno sguardo femminile.
All'improvviso essere cielo,
svanire,
occupare un battito di ciglia
in un colore.
Svegliarsi molteplicità di fiati,
case, città.
Sembra invadersi d'umanità
il corpo ed il suo paesaggio.
Nell'ora in cui
comincia il viaggio
l'anima vuole
una recita cosciente,
un rumore di mani
e realtà sotto le luci.
Applausi incollati
alle fessure di capelli e sipari
sanno.
Solo a metà.

Game of Identity

Game of identity
in a span of masculine voice,
interior movement
of a feminine glance.
Suddenly being sky,
disappearing,
occupying a beat of eyelashes
in a color.
Waking variety of breaths,
houses, cities.
It seems to be invaded by human nature
the body and her landscape.
In the hour in which
the journey begins
the soul wants
a conscious recital,
a din of hands
and reality under the lights.
Round of applause glued
to the cracks of hair and curtains,
they know.
Only half.

Un pugno di mare

Sul limite di un fondale
il suono acerbo
d'un vivere rubato.
Un pugno di mare
risale con i sudori
ed il peso
di deserti stretti
in uno spettro.
È un orrore
la fame e la sete
che in un battello
inizia la sua fine.

A Fistful of Sea

On the boundary of an ocean floor
the unripe sound
of a life stolen.
A fistful of sea
returns with sweat
and the weight
of narrow deserts
in a ghost.
It is a terror
the hunger and the thirst
that in a dinghy
begins her end.

Il respiro della terra

Continuità di linfe e di zolle
in diari di arie sensibili.
La terra assorbe
disperazione, piogge improvvise,
fantasie umane.
Come madre paziente
si fa specchio dei suoi figli,
veglia complicità di glicine,
soffre al rantolo
di deserti confusi.
Nuda e tormentata,
cicatrizza pugni di ruggine
in respiri di muschio.
Il tempo la sfiora,
la guarda nei margini d'asfalto
tra vita, morte ed altre alleanze.
Dentro un guscio
di rotondità e calore
alterna i suoi semi di mondo
all'avvenire.

Breath of Earth

Continuity of sap and of clods
in diaries of sensitive airs.
The earth absorbs
despair, sudden rains,
human fantasies.
As a patient mother
becomes reflection to her children,
keeps watch over wisteria's complicity,
she suffers with the rasping breath
of confused deserts.
Naked and tormented,
she heals fists of resentment
in breaths of moss.
The time grazes it,
watches it in the margins of asphalt
through life, death, and the next alliance.
Inside a shell
of roundness and heat
it turns her world's seeds
to the future.

Un giappone disperato

Capricci di terra e di mare
a schiacciare rughe di cemento
ed occhi di un mondo troppo affannato.
Torna alle macerie
un silenzio che muore tra la gente,
è acre il corridoio di pelli invase
da carezze d'arie radioattive.
Un Giappone disperato
svuota il suo dolore alla storia.
Abbiamo visto un popolo
scolorire sotto la furia
di un buio estremo,
scalzi, gli ultimi fiati a rovescio
di un cielo in agonia.

A Desperate Japan

Tantrums of earth and of sea
crushing wrinkles of cement
and eyes of a world too anxious.
It returns to the ruins
a silence that dies among people,
it is acrid, the hallway of invaded skins,
from strokes of radioactive airs.
A desperate Japan
empties its pain onto history.
We have seen a people
fading beneath the fury
of a dark extreme,
barefoot, the last breaths to the wrong way
of a sky in agony.

Lampi di guerra

Cerco un ordine ai sensi,
ma lampi di guerra
invadono le ingenuità del mio fiato.
Ho addosso il contorno
di un mondo che sanguina
silenzi incompresi,
il pianto estremo di fratelli
che chiedono di tornare
ad un respiro di vita.
Mi acceca il cumulo di dolore
che affolla
accenti di terra e di mare.
Non dormo.
Tocco un colore d'inferno
e in una veglia d'incroci di ciglia
incido tremori
sotto un fragile pulsare.
Per smettere l'urto di un cielo
che esalta strazi e tormenti,
avvolgo tutto il destino
ad un frammento di sogno
e affido il mio vapore
ad un calore ridente di madre.

Lightnings of War

I look for an order to the feelings,
but lightnings of war
invade the innocence of my breath.
I have charged the contour
of a world that bleeds
misunderstood silences,
the extreme distress of comrades
who demand starting again
at a breath of life.
It blinds me, the accumulation of pain
that crowds
stresses of earth and of sea.
I don't sleep.
I touch a color of hell
and in a vigil of crossing eyelashes
I engrave tremors
under(neath) a fragile pulsing.
In order to stop the assault of a sky
that exalts torment and torture,
I wrap every destiny
to a fragment of dream
and I commit my vapor
to a smiling warmth from mother.

Ho pensato a te, Dio

È tempo di accendere preghiere
a riempire di grazie
qualche itinerario d'anima.
Ho pensato a te, Dio,
quanto poco è il mio senso
di donna
senza l'ossigeno della Tua luce.
I miei midolli risanano
dentro tinte di fede
confessandosi in limpidi ventri di cielo.
Spargo a terra tutto il mio peccato,
atterro sopra una luna e le sue alghe,
torno dove il silenzio
viene ad incontrare le mie penitenze.
Raccolte in volo
le mie vene
pronunciano piogge di vita
ed eterne di meditazione,
credono.

I Have Thought of You, God

It's time for kindling prayers
for filling with grace
some itinerary of the soul.
I have thought of you, God,
how small is my sense
of woman
without the oxygen of your light.
My marrows heal
inside shades of faith
confessing in limpid bellies of sky.
I scatter on the earth all my sin,
I land above a moon and its algae,
I go back where silence
comes out to meet my penances.
Collected in flight
my veins
pronounce rains of life
and eternities of meditation,
they believe.

Il mio crescere donna

Volontà alle radici
e calma superiore all'anima,
il mio crescere donna
sui ventagli di fuoco del tempo.
Forse è desiderio del cielo:
il sangue corre
e m'aiuta a scoprire amore
d'aurore.
Inseguo grumi di luce
e silenzi fraterni,
nei miei passi un trovarsi
d'infanzie e paradisi disabitati.
Io tento con forza
un cammino
e grido per incontrare vita
alla morte.

My Growing Woman

Will to the roots
and calm superior to spirit,
my growing woman
on the fans of time's fire.
Maybe it is the desire of the sky:
the blood runs
and it helps me to discover the love
of sunrises.
I chase lumps of light
and brotherly silences,
in my steps a meeting
of childhoods and paradises uninhabited.
I try with strength
a way
and I shout to encounter life
at death.

La mia pelle vede

La mia pelle vede
come quando l'aria
esplora le linfe.
Voglio precipitare
sulle tue linee maschili,
forzare le ginocchia
e scoprire il paese,
il piacere
e la sua forza.

My Skin Sees

My skin sees
as when air
explores sap.
I want to collapse
on your masculine contours,
force the knees
and discover the place,
the pleasure
and its strength.

Quotidiano rifiorire

Mi ripeto che la vita
è un quotidiano rifiorire
come un miracolo senza pudore.
Esulto al suo genuino calore,
a questa luce avuta in dono
al primo respiro.
Tra il corpo e superfici
di cielo,
piena di senso
annuncio la mia volontà
a trasformare
ogni croce in amore.

Daily Blooming

I repeat to myself that life
is a daily blooming
as a miracle without modesty.
I rejoice at its genuine warmth,
to this light had as a gift
to the first breath.
Between the body and surfaces
of heaven,
flood of meaning
I announce my will
to transforming
each cross to love.

Matura il silenzio

Matura il silenzio
in un mare
che regge i miei sguardi
come terra che dolcemente
sostiene umane miserie.
Si rifugia nell'acqua
la carne della mia mente.
Nei limpidi muscoli
della profondità
trovo la forza
di una feconda ragione.
La vita sta
tra un sacrificio
e la purezza delle mie schiume.

Silence Matures

Silence matures
in a sea
that bears my glances
like earth that gently
bears human misery.
The flesh of my mind
takes refuge in the water.
In the limpid muscles
of the depth
I find the strength
of a prolific reason.
Life lingers
between a sacrifice
and the purity of my foam.

Meditazioni al femminile

Mi scopro
in una gradevole epidermide
insieme ad arterie e volontà preziose.
Non mi curo del tempo
e del silenzio
che entrano come pioggia.
Il cielo e l'amore
appagano il mio fiato
dopo un privilegio
divino alla vita.

Meditations in the Feminine

In a pleasant skin
I find myself
together with arteries,
with precious desire.
I do not care for time
or for the silence
that enters like rain.
The sky and the love
satisfy my breath
after a privilege
divine to life.

Troppo breve

Troppo breve il senso
e la natura di un respiro.
Siamo un piccolo brusio
sotto le eternità.
Il mondo come la vita
si affacciano rapidi
dentro le vene,
finchè una polvere
s'impossessa d'ogni radice
e si fa memoria
che abbandona la sua patria.

Too brief

Too brief the sense
and the nature of a breath.
We are a small buzzing
underneath eternities.
The world like life
appears like rapids
inside the veins,
until dust
seizes each of the roots
and becomes memory
that abandons its origin.

Senza patria apparente

Il mare silenziosamente vede
il passo senza patria apparente
di pelli scure,
frotte di straniere ossa
che attraversano il seme dell'estate
in un tardo settembre.
Si sente un fiato all'affanno,
un rimprovero che avanza,
un'eredità di stoffe e collane
che non ha meta.

Without Apparent Origin

The sea silently sees
the footprint without apparent origin
of dark skins,
crowds of foreign bones
which cross the seed of summer
in a late September.
It feels a shortness of breath,
a reproach that advances,
an inheritance of cloths and necklaces
that has no destination.

MICHELA ZANARELLA è poetessa, autrice teatrale e giornalista della FL International Press, è redattrice di Periodico italiano e Laici.it. Ha diretto la collana di poesia ARTe MUSE di David and Matthaus. Presidente dell'A. P. S. Le Ragunanze. Il suo ultimo libro è "Le parole accanto" (Interno Poesia, 2017). Molte sue poesie figurano in antologie a tiratura nazionale e internazionale. La sua poesia è tradotta in inglese, francese, arabo, spagnolo, rumeno, serbo, portoghese e giapponese. Ha ottenuto il Creativity Prize al Premio Internazionale Naji Naaman's 2016. È ambasciatrice per la cultura nel mondo e rappresenta l'Italia in Libano per FGC. È direttrice della Writers Capital International Foundation.

MICHELA ZANARELLA is a poet, playwright, and journalist for the FL International press, as well as an author for Periodico Italiano magazine and Laici.it. She has directed the series of poetry ARTeMUSE published by David and Matthaus. She is President of the association A. P. S. Ragunanze. Zanarella's most recent book is "Le parole accanto" (Interno Poesia, 2017). Many of Zanarella's poems appear in anthologies with national and international circulation. Her poetry has been translated into English, French, Arabic, Spanish, Romanian, Serbian, Portugese, and Japanese. Zanarella was awarded the first place international Creativity Prize in Naji Naaman's 2016 Literary Prizes. She is an ambassador for culture in the world and represents Italy in Lebanon for FGC. She also directs the Writers Capital International Foundation.

LEANNE HOPPE holds an MFA in poetry from Boston University, and she works as a teacher, editor, and translator.

Acknowledgments

A million thanks to Rita Cote, who provided feedback and guidance in several of the translations, and to Giulia Herman, who proofread and brought each poem to its fruition—without the both of you, this project wouldn't have been possible. We thank the journals, anthologies, and websites that previously published poems from this collection:

Babel Web Anthology: "Padre" (Fall 2016)

Our Poetry Archive: "I Chain Myself to the Origins," "August's Glances," "Together Beyond" (October 2016)

XXI Century World Literature: "Padre" (Spring 2016)

Tragicamente Rosso by Michela Zanarella: "Tragically Red" (Fall 2015)

Eastern World Newspaper, Uzbekistan: "I Chain Myself to the Origins," "Sparks of Life," and "Tragically Red" (August–September 2015)

Asymptote blog: "Five Poems by Michela Zanarella" (November 2014)

CROSSINGS

AN INTERSECTION OF CULTURES

Crossings is dedicated to the publication of Italian-language literature and translations from Italian to English.

Rodolfo Di Biasio
  Wayfarers Four. Translated by Justin Vitello. 1998. ISBN 1-88419-17-9. Volume 1.

Isabella Morra
  Canzoniere: A Bilingual Edition. Translated by Irene Musillo Mitchell. 1998. ISBN 1-88419-18-6. Volume 2.

Nevio Spadone
  Lus. Translated by Teresa Picarazzi. 1999. ISBN 1-88419-22-4. Volume 3.

Flavia Pankiewicz
  American Eclipses. Translated by Peter Carravetta. Introduction by Joseph Tusiani. 1999. ISBN 1-88419-23-2. Volume 4.

Dacia Maraini
  Stowaway on Board. Translated by Giovanna Bellesia and Victoria Offredi Poletto. 2000. ISBN 1-88419-24-0. Volume5.

Walter Valeri, editor
  Franca Rame: Woman on Stage. 2000. ISBN 1-88419-25-9. Volume 6.

Carmine Biagio Iannace
  The Discovery of America. Translated by William Boelhower. 2000. ISBN 1-88419-26-7. Volume 7.

Romeo Musa da Calice
  Luna sul salice. Translated by Adelia V. Williams. 2000. ISBN 1-88419-39-9. Volume 8.

Marco Paolini & Gabriele Vacis
  The Story of Vajont. Translated by Thomas Simpson. 2000. ISBN 1-88419-41-0. Volume 9.

Silvio Ramat
  Sharing A Trip: Selected Poems. Translated by Emanuel di Pasquale. 2001. ISBN 1-88419-43-7. Volume 10.

Raffaello Baldini
  Page Proof. Edited by Daniele Benati. Translated by Adria
  Bernardi. 2001. ISBN 1-88419-47-X. Volume 11.

Maura Del Serra
  Infinite Present. Translated by Emanuel di Pasquale and
  Michael Palma. 2002. ISBN 1-88419-52-6. Volume 12.

Dino Campana
  Canti Orfici. Translated and Notes by Luigi Bonaffini. 2003.
  ISBN 1-88419-56-9. Volume 13.

Roberto Bertoldo
  The Calvary of the Cranes. Translated by Emanuel di Pasquale.
  2003. ISBN 1-88419-59-3. Volume 14.

Paolo Ruffilli
  Like It or Not. Translated by Ruth Feldman and James Laughlin.
  2007. ISBN 1-88419-75-5. Volume 15.

Giuseppe Bonaviri
  Saracen Tales. Translated Barbara De Marco. 2006. ISBN
  1-88419-76-3. Volume 16.

Leonilde Frieri Ruberto
  Such Is Life. Translated Laura Ruberto. Introduction by Ilaria
  Serra. 2010. ISBN 978-1-59954-004-7. Volume 17.

Gina Lagorio
  Tosca the Cat Lady. Translated by Martha King. 2009. ISBN 978-
  1-59954-002-3. Volume 18.

Marco Martinelli
  Rumore di acque. Translated and edited by Thomas Simpson.
  2014. ISBN 978-1-59954-066-5. Volume 19.

Emanuele Pettener
  A Season in Florida. Translated by Thomas De Angelis. 2014.
  ISBN 978-1-59954-052-2. Volume 20.

Angelo Spina
  Il cucchiaio trafugato. 2017. ISBN 978-1-59954-112-9. Volume 21.

www.ingramcontent.com/pod-product-compliance
Lightning Source LLC
LaVergne TN
LVHW041254080426
835510LV00009B/729

9 781599 541105